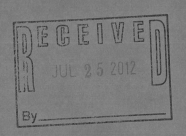

STAT

HOME COURT

STAT

HOME COURT

by *AMAR'E STOUDEMIRE*
illustrated by **TIM JESSELL**

SCHOLASTIC PRESS / NEW YORK

To my children,
Ar'e, Amar'e Jr., Assata,
and all the children of the world.

And to my brother Hazell,
I will always miss you. You are the
main reason for my success.
See you in Paradise!

*   *   *

Special thanks to Michael Northrop

ISBN 978-0-545-43169-9

Text copyright © 2012 by Amar'e Stoudemire Enterprises
Illustrations copyright © 2012 by Scholastic Inc.

Cover and interior art by Tim Jessell
Original cover design by Yaffa Jaskoll

12 11 10 9 8 7 6 5 4 3 2 1   12 13 14 15 16 17/0

Printed in the U.S.A.   23

First printing, August 2012

CHAPTER 1

The wheels of the skateboard made a rumbling hum as they rolled over the pavement at the little town park. I loved that sound. The world rushed by me as I zipped across the blacktop. I could feel how smooth or rough it was right through my sneakers, and it was like I was watching the park in fast-forward. The greens and browns of the grass and trees flashed by on the sides as I kept my eyes on the little concrete path in front of me, looking for the next good, flat spot. I was trying to get this one trick down, but the board wasn't cooperating. It slipped out from under me again and went bouncing across the ground.

That had been happening to me a lot lately, and I knew why. I'd had a big growth spurt this year. We're talking, like, my pants from before looked like shorts on me now. I was definitely the tallest eleven-year-old in my neighborhood, and it could be pretty tough to keep all my long limbs going in the same direction as those four little wheels. Put it this way: When I bent down to pick up the board, I had to bend a long way.

I was trying to do an ollie. What you do is pop the board into the air while you're riding it. If you do it right, it's like you're jumping with the board glued to your feet — pretty cool. I was still only doing it right about half the time, so I stayed on the path and worked on it a little longer.

My jumps were getting a little higher, and I decided to head for a bigger stretch of pavement to work on them.

"Ay-yo!" I heard as I turned a corner. I thought I might be in trouble, but when I looked up, I could see it was just the opposite. It was my friend Mike. He was on the park's old basketball court with our friend Deuce.

"What's up?" I called. This was our local court, and the three of us had spent whole days playing here together.

As I kick-turned my board onto the little walkway that led to it, they went back to playing one-on-one. I could see by the way they were moving that they'd probably been out there for a few hours already. They were going a little slower, and I could see the sun shining off some sweat on their foreheads. Deuce never went too slow for long, though. I was almost to the court when I saw him give Mike a shoulder fake and then turn on the jets. He was at the hoop in a heartbeat. Deuce wasn't a big kid, but he was fast. His first step was like a striking cobra.

"Where'd you go?" Mike shouted as Deuce turned the corner on him.

"Disappeared," said Deuce, once he'd laid the ball up and in. "Don't you know I'm magic?"

"I know you're lucky," Mike said as he took the ball out.

Right away, Mike started backing his way in toward the basket for an easy shot. Mike was almost as tall as me and much taller than Deuce. I was looking forward to overhearing some good trash talk. It was Deuce's best defense. But Mike caught sight of me at the edge of the court and picked up his dribble.

"Well, well, well," said Mike. "Look who finally made it. Get over here, Amar'e!"

"Yeah, get over here and help me D up this clown!" called Deuce.

"Neither of you can stop me down low," bragged Mike.

The sun was getting kind of low now, but come on, that was a direct challenge! I had to accept. I'd be good as long as I got home in time for dinner. My dad definitely had some ground rules, and being home on time was right up there at the top of the list. I don't know how much he had paid for his watch, but whatever it was, he got his money's worth because he was always checking it. He was never late himself, so he expected the same from me. He was fair, but tough.

"All right, all right," I called. Like I said: It was a direct challenge. And I was hoping it wouldn't take too long to win. "I got this, no problem."

"This kid's cocky for a skater," said Deuce.

I had to laugh: I walked right into that one. Deuce and Mike high-fived, and I waved them off. It was good to see my friends. Mike bounced a skip pass to me as I stepped onto the court. I sprinted over and took the ball at a full run. A few quick dribbles and I laid it up. They let me take a few shots to warm up. But when I bricked my third jumper, Deuce swooped in and grabbed the rebound.

"What were you doing all this time?" he said. He zipped by me, dribbling low like he always did. He had a good handle and hated turning the ball over.

"Working on a trick," I said. "I was over where those flat paths come together. It's good for skating."

He nodded. Lake Wales, Florida, was a really small town. We all knew it pretty well by now, and we probably knew every inch of this park. The paths I was skating on are the same ones where we used to ride bikes. But that didn't mean Deuce accepted my excuse. "We've been here since school got out," he said. "There were some other kids, too. They were pretty good. We could've used your skills, man."

I put my hands up for the ball, but Deuce passed it to Mike instead. Mike clanged one off the front of the rim, but the rebound went right to him. He drained a shot from the same spot. Then he looked over.

"There were already three dudes from our class when we got here, so we had to play two-on-two and I wound up sitting out twice," he said. "You *know* I hate sitting out."

It was true. Mike loved to play basketball so much that he got really annoyed when he had to sit and watch other people do it.

"Sorry, Mike," I said. I held up my hands again and he passed me the ball. "If that was right after school, I was still doing homework anyway."

"Man, Amar'e," said Mike. "I don't know why they stuck such a nerd brain into such a baller body."

Deuce laughed. "What are you laughing at?" I said. "You study more than I do!"

"That's right," he said. "They don't put just anyone on the honor roll."

"Yeah," I said. "I'm *honor* roll with my homework and *on a* roll when I skate."

They both laughed at my joke. Well, okay, maybe it was more like they groaned.

"All right, high roller," said Deuce. "Let's see if you remember how to get that thing in the hoop."

They both got down into defensive positions in front of me. Mike clapped his hands a few times: *Bap-Bap-Bap!* I dribbled the ball hard in response: *Bomp Bomp Bomp!* We may have gotten off to a late start, but it was game on now. I dribbled hard to the left, to get Deuce in between Mike and me. With the smaller defender on me, I raised up and drained a rainbow jumper. The ball clipped the back of the metal rim as it banged through the hoop. I loved that sound, too.

I got really into the game after that. It wasn't until we finished that I realized how long we'd been playing. *Oh, man*, I thought. *I'm gonna be late!*

I looked up at the sun, just above the treetops. It was like I was looking at my dad's angry face, staring right at me. I had to get home now!

CHAPTER 2

*B*etween skateboarding, basketball, hanging with my friends, and all the other things I liked to do after school, I didn't have enough time as it was. I definitely didn't want to get grounded.

Now that board was my only hope to get home before it was too late.

"I gotta jet," I said.

"Yeah, me too," said Mike. "See you guys at school tomorrow."

"Later," said Deuce.

They both took off. Mike lived closest, which was a good thing since he didn't have a skateboard like me or sprinter speed like Deuce. I plunked the board down on the sidewalk and got moving. The little town rolled by, but not fast enough. Some days I tapped each mailbox I passed, just to keep things interesting. Today I was all business. I had one foot on the board, and I was kicking hard with the other.

There's a stretch near my house with no sidewalk, so I took a deep breath and veered off into the little bike lane on the road. I was doing a good job of staying inside the white line, at least when it wasn't too faded to see. But I was rushing and probably not looking around as much as I should have been. A beat-up brown car shot past me a little too close.

"Watch it!" I said, kicking hard toward the curb.

"*BRawEEerEEP!*" went its broken-down horn.

Close call.

I kept my eyes peeled, and the most I had to deal with the rest of the way were a few rough spots in the sidewalk and one angry poodle. I finally reached the house. The front light was on, so I knew Dad was waiting for me inside. I grabbed my board and hustled toward the door.

As soon as I pushed it open, I could smell the pizza.

It was my favorite dinner. It was my favorite lunch, too, and I was definitely open to the idea of having it for breakfast! But I was running late, so I had to hope that more than just the smell was left. My dad and older bro were both big, strong guys, and they could both eat. Let me put it this way: If you were a pepperoni pizza, you wouldn't want to be left alone in a room with them for more than three seconds.

I zoomed through the kitchen and heard a plate clink in the living room. I panicked for a second, thinking they might already be clearing the table. But I turned the corner and saw my dad just sitting down. His plate was in front of him, and the pizza box was in the center of the table, not even opened. Phew!

"You made it just in time," said my dad, Hazell.

The pizza smell had taken over my brain for a while there, but the way he said "just in time" reminded me I was late.

"I know, I know," I said. There was no sense in denying it, but changing the subject seemed worth a shot. I took a deep breath and added: "I didn't know we were having pizza."

"What?" said Dad. "We've got to have a pie to get you home on time?"

I put both my hands up in front of me, like *Okay, you got me.* I snuck a look over at my older brother, Junior. He was loving this — like brothers usually do when they're not the one who's in trouble!

"Yeah," said Dad, "while you got those hands up, you better go and wash 'em. Looks like you might have some basketball court on there."

When I got back from the bathroom, my hands were clean and my stomach was empty. I was ready to eat, but first I had to find out how mad Dad was. I really hoped I wasn't grounded.

"You know you're late, right?" he said.

"Yes, Dad," I said.

"And you know how hard it is to keep this one from eating everything in sight as soon as it arrives?" he said.

He hooked a thumb over toward Junior, who just rolled his eyes.

I was expecting Dad to let me have it now, but instead, his shoulders and face both kind of dropped. "But I've had enough trouble today," he said.

He'd had a long day already, and I felt bad for making it a little longer.

"You going to be on time the rest of the week?" he asked, looking back up.

"Yeah," I said. "I promise."

"All right, then," he said. "Consider this a warning."

"Thanks, Dad," I said.

Dad had his own lawn-care company, so a good day was one where it didn't rain, none of the equipment broke, and he got paid at the end. A bad day could be just about anything else.

"Something happen at work today?" I asked.

"Just that there was too much of it," he said.

For a second, I thought he might leave it at that, but it turns out he did have something he wanted to get off his chest.

"Me and the guys did a real nice job on a place over by the park this morning," he said. "Whole lawn was picture-perfect when we left. But by the time the folks who owned it got home, someone had come by and messed it all up. Left garbage out front, walked right through the bushes, stepped on some flowers, you name it."

"Who was it?" I said.

"Don't know," he said. "They acted like a herd of buffalo, but it was probably just some troublemakers. Looks like they were just cutting through the yard or something, but it's the third time this's happened in the last week."

"Not cool," said Junior.

"Seriously," I said.

"Had to clean it up for free," said Dad, "but at least the customers paid up for the work this morning." We didn't have a lot of money but my dad worked hard for what he earned. He was proud of that.

It would also explain the pizza. He must've bought it on the way home to cheer himself up.

"Anyway," he said, "let's eat."

He reached over and opened the pizza box. The smell of fresh, hot pizza came out in a cloud. It sort of blew all the troubles away, at least for a little while. We dug in. Man, that first bite of hot pizza! And the second! Bite after bite of warm crust and melted cheese disappeared into my mouth.

For a few minutes, the only sound was chewing. Then it was time to reload. My brother and I both reached for the same slice. His hand was bigger and it boxed mine out.

"You earned it," I said.

"Yeah," he said, pulling his hand back, "but you got more growing to do."

We both smiled, but I reached in fast, before he changed his mind.

"Got some quick hands there, STAT," said my dad. He'd been waiting to get another slice himself.

STAT was my dad's nickname for me. It stood for Standing Tall And Talented. That's how he wanted me to act and who he wanted me to be, so he called me that a lot. That's who I wanted to be, too, and right then, it felt like we were all on the same page.

Junior and I were living here with Dad right now. We split time between Florida with Dad and New York with my mom. I liked it here — even when it wasn't pizza night — but I was also looking forward to visiting Mom and my half brother up there in a few weeks. Junior was five years older than me, so things were a little different for him. But mostly I think he felt the same way. And anyway, New York was nice this time of year. It was a lot cooler, that was for sure.

After dinner, I had some more homework to do. I had to finish the day-to-day stuff before I went out after school. That was Dad's rule, and he controlled the pizza. But this was a big paper for history. It was due in a week and it looked like I'd need all that time to do it.

I looked over the assignment again. I had to write about one figure from history and say how he inspires me and what he means to my everyday life. There was a long list of people to choose from, but one popped out right away: Dr. Martin Luther King, Jr. I already knew some things about him — the stuff pretty much everyone knows — and I wanted to learn more.

History was my favorite subject, but this was a big topic. I mean, where do you even start with a guy like that? I got out my history book and started reading. There was a lot of stuff about him in a big chapter on the U.S. civil rights movement. Yep, that's what I wanted to write about: Dr. King and the civil rights movement.

I still wasn't sure where to start, though. Maybe I just needed some food for thought.

I walked out to the kitchen and opened the refrigerator. There were only two slices of pizza left. One was thin, and the other was almost as wide as two slices put together. My big brother was sitting at the table, drinking a glass of milk.

"Don't even think about it," he said when I reached for the bigger slice.

I took the little slice for myself and brought the big one over to him.

"Writing a paper on Martin Luther King," I said.

"I did that, too," he said. "So did just about everyone else in my class."

He was right: Everyone would pick Dr. King off that list. I'd have to figure out a way to make my paper stand out if I wanted a good grade.

"Thanks," I said.

"For what?" he said through a mouth full of pizza: Furr whuh?

I finished my microslice and went back to my room for my next assignment. The next day was Friday, the last day of school for the week. I always tried to dress well, but especially on Fridays. When that last bell went off, I wanted to start the weekend in style! I didn't always make the best decisions first thing in the morning, so I decided to pick my outfit in advance.

I looked over my options. It's all about the shoes. I checked out my sneaker collection and narrowed it down pretty quickly to two: my best new pair of red-and-black kicks and a pair of old-school white high-tops that I brought out on special occasions. I decided to go old-school, because if Friday isn't a special occasion, I don't know what is.

With white kicks, I needed color somewhere else. I got it with a red polo shirt that had a white collar to match my sneakers and was just my size. I like my shirts to really fit, not stop a few inches above my wrists or look like a tent just collapsed on top of me. I finished it all off with a good pair of dark jeans. I looked the outfit over and shook my head: I was good to go!

CHAPTER 3

I sat with my normal crew at lunch on Friday: Deuce, Mike, Tavoris, and Marcus. Tavoris is quiet and serious most of the time; he was wearing a button-up shirt. Marcus is a motormouth; he was in a worn-out Dolphins T-shirt. They were total opposites but they made a good team. They must've thought so, too, because they'd been best friends since forever.

"That's a fresh outfit," said Mike when I plunked down my tray to join them.

"Thanks," I said. "Just something I threw together."

They didn't need to know I'd done the throwing last night, and there was bigger news anyway.

"Hey," said Tavoris, leaning forward. You could tell he

had something good. "There's a big hoops tournament. Marcus and I just signed up."

"Oh, yeah?" said Mike. "What's it called? Where'd you sign up?"

"Sign-up sheet's in the hallway," said Tavoris. "Name's at the top."

That's just the way Tavoris was: He never said much more than he needed to. Marcus was the guy who you could count on to give you the scoop.

Deuce knew that. He turned to Marcus and said, "So?"

Sure enough, Marcus started telling us all about it. He remembered the name of the tournament, exactly where the sign-up sheet was, and even the names of some of the kids who'd already signed up.

"Stevie's on there; he's the first name," he said. "And Manny, Omar, and Ray, too."

Those guys were all really serious ballers. They were probably practicing together already. I got kind of a bad feeling. A tournament like that would take tons of time. I thought about all the other things I liked to do on the weekend: skateboarding, playing baseball and football around the neighborhood, maybe bowling with Junior.

And I thought about all the things I had to do on top of that, too: work with my dad, homework. How was I supposed to fit a tournament in there?

"I'm signing up as soon as we get out of here," said Mike.

"You know I'm down," said Deuce.

"What about you, Amar'e?" said Marcus.

Everyone at the table was looking at me now. I squirmed in my seat, trying to think of something to say. I didn't want to say no to my friends, but I didn't really want to say yes either. Finally, I thought of something.

"That reminds me," I said. "I heard a pretty good joke."

The table was quiet. Everyone was still looking at me. Mike was the first to say something. "Yeah?" he said. He never could resist a new joke.

"S'it funny?" asked Marcus.

It was off the hook.

"Okay, check it," I said, trying to remember how the joke started. "These two friends are both huge ball fans, but one of them isn't so bright. You might want to pay extra attention to that part, Mike."

Mike just waved me off like he always does.

"Anyway," I said, "they're visiting a big basketball museum with their families. They're in the part of the museum that shows the best teams from the 1970s, so there are framed pictures of all these teams, right?"

I looked around to make sure everyone was still with me.

"Yeah," said Mike.

"Okay," said Marcus.

"Sure," said Tavoris.

I knew I didn't have to worry about Deuce getting lost, so I went on. "And under each picture, it says, like, '70–'71, '71–'72, and all the way up to '78–'79. So the first kid is looking at all the crazy seventies styles, like the short-shorts and pulled-up tube socks, and the second kid turns to him and says — you guys ready?"

"Yeah, yeah," said Marcus. "What'd he say?"

"He said, 'I can't believe all these teams lost by one point!'"

They all busted out laughing. I did, too, but part of that was relief.

"Oh, man!" said Mike.

"That is one dumb kid!" said Tavoris.

After lunch, Mike, Deuce, and I headed to history class.

"Man," said Mike. "I'm going to have to work on this paper all weekend. Four pages? That's like a book!"

"You haven't even started it yet, have you?" said Deuce.

"Of course not," said Mike. "I got all weekend!"

"Man, Mike," I said, shaking my head, "you are hopeless."

"Yeah, just 'cause you two are probably halfway done," he said.

"Not halfway," said Deuce.

"Nah, me neither," I said.

"You started, though, right?" said Deuce.

"Yeah," I said. "I picked my topic and did some reading."

"Yeah, same here," said Deuce. "Who you writing about?"

"MLK, all the way," I said.

"Yeah, me too," said Deuce.

"Me three," said Mike. "Those other names are ancient anyway."

"I just can't figure out that last part: What he means to my life," I said. "I can't just say what he means to everyone — especially since the whole class is probably picking him. You know Ms. Bourne is always on us about 'originality.' I need to figure out something that's just about me."

"Yeah, me too," said Deuce. "That's the tough part."

"Ha!" said Mike. "Bourne got you two nerds good!"

"Yo, Mike," I said. "You've got to do it, too."

"Oh, yeah," he said.

When we turned the last corner heading to class, I saw the big bulletin board in the hallway. I got that same feeling again, like I was cornered.

"Here it is, just like Marcus said," said Mike, pointing to a long sheet of yellow paper.

"'Lake Wales Youth Basketball Tournament,'" read Deuce. "'A Wale of a Tourney.' Sweet!"

It was a sign-up sheet. There was a pen hanging from a string next to it. Mike had already picked it up and started signing his name. As soon as he was done, Deuce grabbed the pen and signed his. When he was done, he held the pen out for me.

"Still a few spots left," he said, a big smile on his face. "Hope we can be on the same team."

I didn't take the pen.

"'Sup, man?" he said.

"I don't know," I said. I really wished I had another new joke. All I could think to say was, "A tournament?"

My brother had played in some of these, maybe even in this same one. There was a lot involved: practices, waiting around between rounds, and a ton of games, everything from preliminary to championship and maybe even a "consolation round" for third place.

"Yeah," said Mike. "A tournament!"

"This could take, you know, days," I said.

I was thinking of the next trick I wanted to learn on my skateboard, and those baseball and football games around the neighborhood. I was thinking of all that stuff. . . .

"Yeah," said Deuce. "Days of playing hoops. Days of winning!"

"I don't know," I said again. "People there are going to be really serious about it. You know I just like to play for fun. . . ."

I was feeling the pressure. It was tough to say no to my friends, especially when they were so into it. Deuce was still holding the pen out, but right then the warning bell went off.

"Uh-oh," he said. He let the pen drop, and we all hustled toward class. *Saved by the bell*, I thought, but I could see he was disappointed. I could see they both were, and I felt bad.

"Let's play after school. We'll change clothes and head over to the court," I said as we headed toward the door.

They both gave me quick looks.

"That's more like it!" said Mike.

"Yeah, we can talk about this there," said Deuce.

"Maybe," I said. "If I'm not too busy dropping thirty points!"

"In your dreams!" said Deuce.

"And your nightmares!" I said.

We made it to class with two seconds to spare, but we were all smiling when we got there.

CHAPTER 4

*"M*an," said Mike. "It looks like the tournament has already started."

"Yeah," said Deuce. "The NCAA tournament."

The kids crowding the court weren't really college age, but they probably looked that way to five-foot-nothing Deuce. The side closest to us had three big kids on it, really going at it. They were definitely older, and all three were pretty tall. If I had to guess, I'd say they were in eighth or even ninth grade. It looked like one of them had the beginnings of a mustache.

The other court had a hoop with an old, bent rim, and it was full of parents with their little kids anyway. We'd come all the way there, and we didn't want to play P-I-G with first graders, so the older kids were our only option. We watched them play for a while. They were playing hard enough that you could hear their arms slap against each other when they crashed the boards for a rebound.

"Maybe we should just come back tomorrow," said Deuce.

"Nah, just be cool," said Mike.

"They'll probably let us mix in with them," I said. "Or maybe they're leaving soon."

The tallest player missed a long three. The ball hit the side of the rim and bounced toward where we were standing along the side of the court. Mike grabbed it before it could roll too far away.

"Can we get in there?" he said, before throwing the ball back to them.

Their tallest guy grabbed the pass.

"Hold up, guys," he said to his friends. Then he began sort of sauntering over toward us. He was a decent player, and he knew it. The other two followed him over. He dribbled the ball slowly, and you could see him sizing us up. As he looked at Deuce, he made a little sound, like half a laugh. That made me kind of mad, and I bet Deuce wasn't too happy about it either.

"He's fast," I said. "Lightning fast."

"Yeah?" said the big guy. He was standing in front of me now.

"Yeah," I said, standing straighter.

He reached up and sort of scratched his chin with his hand, making a show of thinking it over. He sized me up again, and I stood as tall as I could. We were almost eye to eye. He ran the tip of his index finger over his mini-mustache. He had me there. He gave one more quick look over at Mike and Deuce.

"Nah," he said. "Come back in a few years, kids."

"Yeah," said one of the others. "We might be done with the court by then."

Those two fist-bumped as they turned and headed back toward the hoop. Then the third one had to take his shot at us. "Feel free to stay there and keep throwing the ball back to us!"

And just like that, they went back to their game.

"Jerks," said Deuce.

He said it loudly, but not loud enough for them to hear him. They were jerks, but they were *big* jerks.

"Yeah, bunch of clowns," said Mike.

"Is that a mustache or did he just drink a peach-fuzz milkshake?" I said.

They could've at least let us mix in. Three-on-three is much better than playing one-on-two and alternating possessions, like they were doing now. We watched them for a while, but it just made us want to play more.

"I guess we could dribble around on the side over there," said Mike.

That didn't sound so great either. I looked over at my board and helmet, and then looked over at the road. There was a decent curb where I could work on my boardslide.

"Nah," I said. "I'm gonna take my board and work on some stuff. Not really room for all three of us along the side there anyway."

"Okay," said Mike. "That's cool."

"All right," said Deuce. "What can you do, right?"

As I was heading down to the road, I saw a kid named Roger heading toward the court. He was a year younger, but a decent guy, with a sweet jump shot. We'd played hoops with him before. If the other kids weren't there, we could've run two-on-two.

"Older kids are hogging the court," I said. "And it's kindergarten on the other side."

"Sucks," said Roger.

"Yep," I said.

We fist-bumped as we passed, then I switched my attention to the road, looking for a good stretch of curb. Once I found one, I got right to it. The idea is pretty simple: You get up some speed, and then try to sort of pop the board up and sideways onto the curb, so that the bottom of the board is sliding along it. I buckled up my helmet because, I mean, count the things that could go wrong, right? Then I took a few slow tries at it.

It was harder than I thought it would be. I wiped out the first two times. I made sure I fell forward into the grass both times. But I like a challenge, so I guess I got pretty into it. Next thing I knew, it was an hour later. The underside of my board and my own underside were both a little scratched up, but I was starting to get the hang of it.

When I finally looked up at the court, I was surprised to see Mike, Deuce, and Roger playing the older kids, three-on-three. I grabbed my board and headed up there to see what was up, but there wasn't much left to see.

I got there just in time to see the tallest guy on the court, ol' Fuzzy Mustache, seriously rejecting the youngest one. Roger landed hard on his butt after the blocked shot, and the older kids grabbed the ball and scored easily. I guess it was game point, because as soon as it went in, my friends started walking off the court.

"Uncool!" said Mike.

"What happened?" I said, but in my heart, I already knew. Over their shoulders, I could see the older kids laughing and bumping their forearms together to congratulate each other. Meanwhile, Mike, Deuce, and Roger looked seriously beaten down.

"Three-on-three," confirmed Deuce. "They magically 'changed their minds' as soon as you took your wheelie-dealie there down to the road."

I looked down at my skateboard. I should've known. When they sized us up before, they didn't decide not to play us because we were too young. It was because Mike and I were pretty much their size, and I'd already told them how fast Deuce was. They were afraid they'd lose to three younger kids.

"Well, that stunk," said Roger, kicking the grass.

No offense to him, but he's a year younger and a foot shorter than me. Once he showed up, I guess they liked their odds a lot better.

"So they . . ." I started. I didn't know exactly how to put it.

"They let us have it," said Mike.

"Yeah," said Deuce. "They went all out, knocked into us, pushed us around, and didn't give us any foul calls. It was ridiculous."

"They're just . . . you know," said Roger, looking back over his shoulder at the older kids.

"Yeah, I know," I said. "They're butchers."

"That's the word," said Deuce. "Anyway, I'm heading home. Gotta get some ice on this knee."

"Yeah, me too," said Mike. "Gotta get some ice on this, well, all of me."

"Wow, guys," I said. "Sorry about that. I didn't know. . . ."

"S'okay, Amar'e," said Deuce.

"Yeah," said Mike.

"Not your fault," said Roger.

And maybe it wasn't, but I still felt bad seeing them like this, beat-up and beat down at the same time.

"Yeah!" I called out to try to get the bullies' attention. Then I pointed over to the little kids on the other side of the court, still trying to get to P-I-G with their folks. "Maybe you can play them next!"

They didn't even bother to look over. All I could do was walk with the guys down to the sidewalk. I had to slow up because I was the only one without some kind of a limp.

Once I got back home, I tried to calm down and forget about it by doing some more of that history project. I was looking forward to finishing up my reading on the civil rights movement. I read all about Martin Luther King, Jr., and the power of nonviolence. Those kids on the court could learn a thing or two from him.

CHAPTER 5

"**R**ise and grind!" said my older brother.

In case I missed it, he clapped his hands next to my head. I cracked my eyes open. Sunlight was streaming into the room and he was standing next to my bed.

"Come on, man," I groaned, "it's Saturday!"

I wrapped the pillow around my ears and turned back over. I knew from experience that he wasn't going away. He was up and dressed, and that meant that it was time for me to get going, too.

CLAP CLAP CLAP!

"All right, all right," I said, throwing the covers back. I had to get up anyway, but I wouldn't have minded doing it on my own, without sound effects.

I was halfway through watching my second cartoon — and all the way through my second bowl of cereal — when Dad came into the room. "Better get ready," he said.

"Already ready!" I reported.

I had my work clothes on: just some old shorts and a T-shirt that had seen better days. Sometimes I helped Dad out with his lawn-care company. It worked out for both of us: He got an extra set of hands, and I got some spending money. I took my cereal bowl to the kitchen and then followed him out to the truck.

"Gonna be a hot one," he said.

I looked up and felt the sun already strong on my face. He was right, but I knew he didn't mind. He liked it here in Florida and liked being outdoors. As for me, I was just glad I'd gone with the shorts.

"We've got to make a few stops," said Dad as he double-checked the hitch on the trailer that had the mowers in it. There were riding mowers for the other workers, a smaller push mower for me, and a bunch of other stuff, like rakes and a bucket of work gloves and gardening equipment.

"Yeah?" I said.

"Yep," he said. "Got the whole crew working today."

"Where are we working?" I asked.

"One of the big places, right on the lake," he said.

"Nice," I said.

We climbed into the cab of the truck. I lowered the window on my side, and rested my arm there, letting my elbow hang out into the sun. I knew we'd be picking up a few of the guys and I'd have to scootch all the way over next to Dad when we did, but for now I was riding shotgun.

"Try not to take up too much space over there," said Dad, noticing how comfortable I was making myself.

"Like father, like son," I said.

A quick laugh rumbled up from his big chest, and he turned the key to start the truck.

I was the last person out when we got to the house where we were working. That's what happens when you end up squished in the middle. I walked around to stretch out my legs as Dad started talking business with the guy who owned the home.

I guess there was a lot of business to talk about because my legs were good and stretched out before their mouths were anywhere close to shut. I decided to walk around to the other side of the big yellow house and take a look at the main lawn.

First of all, it was a long walk. These big houses right on the lake were something else: three floors and who knows how many rooms. Second, it was worth the trip. I turned the corner and saw a huge green lawn, sloping down and ending in the blue water of the lake. It was just green and blue, stretched out in front of me.

"Any problems?" I heard behind me.

I whirled around like I was coming off a screen and looking for a pass, but it was just my dad.

"What d'ya mean, Pops?" I said.

"The way you were looking around, I thought that same herd of buffalo might've come through here," he said.

"You mean whoever's been messing up lawns lately?" I said.

"Yep." We both took another quick look around the lawn.

"Doesn't look like it," I said.

"Nope," he said. "All I see is a whole lot of grass in need of mowing."

Right on cue, I heard the sound of one of the big riding mowers coming around the side of the house. Dad heard it, too, and it kicked him back into Big Boss mode.

"Well, I'm not paying you to stand here gawking," he said. "Fire up that push mower and get started on the front."

"All right, all right," I said, heading back the way I'd come.

Dad continued to shout instructions as I went: "Make sure you get down by the road — but watch out for the mailbox! And those rose bushes!"

That was always my job. I mowed around the front, taking extra care to avoid the garden and shrubs and all that other stuff that those turbocharged riding mowers were liable to run right over. I'd gotten pretty good at it: cutting the grass and leaving the rest. I was like a specialist: Secret Agent Double-Mow-Seven!

Back out front, I gave the cord two good, hard tugs and the mower started right up. After that I got right to work. All I could hear was the *BRRRRRRMMM* of the engine, and all I could smell was the fresh-cut grass. Between that and the sun beating down on my head, I started to zone out a little. I kept thinking about that big back lawn.

It looked like an acre or maybe two, and right now Dad and his guys were mowing all that tall grass as neat and trim as any barber ever could. And at the end of it, there was the lake with a little wooden dock and a boat tied up at the end. Wouldn't it be amazing to have a house like that myself someday?

I caught a flash of red in front of me — it was the hat of a brightly painted garden gnome. I turned the mower just in time to avoid running it over.

"Phew!" I said.

That was close. Running over that little statue would have been bad for it, worse for the mower, and worst of all for me! I needed to get my head back in the game before I committed gnome-icide.

For the rest of the job, I kept my eyes down just like I did when I was skating over an extra-bumpy stretch of sidewalk. The only other thing I let myself think about was what I'd do with the money I was earning. Maybe the movies . . . or a new pair of kicks . . . I'd definitely get some music. As the day got longer, the grass got shorter.

I was mowing the last few feet of grass, down by the road, when I saw it. Someone had taken an empty soda can, twisted it so the metal was bent, and then crushed it flat. Then they'd just dropped it on the lawn. A few feet later, someone had kicked a little hunk of grass up. Next to that, there was a candy wrapper hanging from a bush like a chocolate-smeared earring.

The sidewalk was just a few feet away, but whoever did this had kicked up this guy's lawn anyway. And there was a trashcan on the corner, but they'd used the lawn for that, too. I threw out the wrapper and the crushed-up can. Then I put the little wedge of grass back in place and pressed it down, just like the golfers do on TV. I decided not to tell my dad. I knew it would just make him mad. No need to ruin a good day.

CHAPTER 6

"**H**ey, hey, can you drop me off here?" I said to Dad as we turned the corner in his truck. We were headed home after finishing up the job, and we'd already dropped the other two guys off.

"What, right here on the side of the road?" he said, and then he saw them too. "Those your boys?"

"Yeah," I said.

We were rolling right up on Mike and Deuce as they walked down the sidewalk.

"Yeah, all right," said Dad, but instead of slowing down, he started speeding up. When he pulled up even with them, he mashed his hand into the center of the steering wheel.

BREEEEEEEEEP!

The truck's horn was really loud. Mike jumped about two feet in the air, and Deuce froze like a rabbit caught out in the open. Dad was splitting his sides laughing as I climbed down out of the truck, and, okay, maybe I was laughing a little, too.

"Man, you guys," I said. "You should've seen your faces!"

I imitated Deuce's, making my mouth really tiny and my eyes really big.

Then they both got to work insisting that I hadn't seen what I just saw.

"Nah, nah," Mike was saying. "I was just a little surprised, that's all. I definitely wasn't —"

But Dad beeped as he pulled away, and Mike jumped again.

Deuce and I both started laughing at him, and he just slumped down.

"Can't believe I did that," he said, shaking his head.

Once the sound of the big truck faded away, the street was quiet and the three of us were just standing there.

"You definitely know how to make an entrance," said Deuce.

"All my pop's idea," I said. "Where you guys headed?"

"Big baseball game going on over in the park," said Deuce. "Left you a message, but I guess you were getting your mow on. Timmy told me about the game. I think it's mostly his crew."

"Sounds cool," I said. "That what's in the backpack?"

"Yeah, a couple of gloves, a ball, and some other things," said Deuce. His blue backpack was stuffed extra full today. It made him look even smaller than usual.

We headed straight for the park and took all the shortcuts we knew, but the game had already started by the time we got there. Home plate was a flattened-out cardboard box, first base was a Frisbee, and second was an old T-shirt. I pointed to the metal fence post they were using for third. "I hope no one slides in," I said.

"Seriously," said Mike. "Think I'd take the out."

Timmy was Deuce's cousin. He called time when he spotted us, and came over to talk. The first baseman doesn't usually just call time-out like that, but then first base isn't normally a Frisbee either.

"Hey, cuz," said Deuce.

"Hey, Big D," said Timmy.

"Any chance we can get in on this?" said Deuce.

"Yeah, mos def," said Timmy, looking around the field. "We already chose up sides, but we could definitely use another outfielder. That would save us a lot of time chasing the ball. And we could probably use a shortstop, too, now that you mention it."

"I can play in the outfield," I said.

"Yeah, big man," said Timmy. "I know you can."

We fist-bumped. Timmy was a good guy. To tell the truth, Deuce's whole family was pretty solid.

"Can't have all three of you on the same team, though," said Timmy.

"S'all right," said Deuce. "We only have two gloves."

We wound up playing the last five innings. It was a pretty fun game. I know it was good because I had twice as many grass stains on my shorts at the end as when I'd started. That and no one slid into that metal pole at third base.

I was a little beat after that. I mean, I'd spent all morning pushing a lawn mower around in the sun and then played most of a baseball game. But it was Saturday, I was with my best friends, and the sun was still up. There was no way I was going to go home just yet.

"What next, guys?" I said. Lake Wales wasn't a big town, so it's not like we had tons of options. But that didn't matter because, for me and my friends, the answer was always going to be sports.

"Could head over to the court," said Mike as he slipped on the backpack. His team had lost, so he had to carry it for the rest of the day.

"You got a ball in that thing?" I said to Deuce, since it was his pack.

"Don't leave home without it!" he said.

We were all up for it. I hadn't gotten to play at all the day before, and they'd only played one short game against those older kids. And from the looks of them afterward, that had been more like Ultimate Fighting than hoops.

We took our time walking over, just sort of enjoying having the day to ourselves. When we reached the court, they were still busting on me for a fly ball I missed in the outfield. The sun got in my eyes — at least that's what I told them! But when I looked over at the court, I thought I really was having trouble seeing.

"Aww, man," said Deuce.

"What are they doing here?" said Mike.

It was the hacks again. We'd never seen them before yesterday, but there they were for the second straight day, strutting around our local court like they owned it. One of them was scraping the bottom of his sneaker against the wire fence, and another one had just finished off a tall can of iced tea and tossed it at him. They were all shouting and laughing about something.

"What do you think?" said Deuce. "Up for a rematch?"

"I don't know, maybe," said Mike. "I'm still pretty banged up from yesterday, but at least we're at full strength now."

He looked over at me.

"Up to you," I said. I wasn't really at "full strength" after those hours of mowing and innings of baseball. But if my friends wanted a second shot at these guys, I wasn't going to say no.

Mike and Deuce looked at each other. Deuce shrugged. "They probably won't even play the three of us," he said. "They wouldn't yesterday. And I don't see Roger anywhere."

We looked up at the court, and the biggest guy was hanging on the rim after dunking the ball. They were so into themselves that they hadn't noticed us yet.

"Yeah," said Mike. "Probably not. What do you think, Amar'e?"

"Like I said, man, it's up to you guys," I said. "You're the ones who had to put up with their cheap shots. But you know I like to play for fun, and playing these guys today? It just doesn't sound like much fun to me."

"Yeah," said Mike, looking down at the scraped-up knee he got yesterday. "Definitely not much fun."

So it was a mutual decision. We weren't scared of those guys. We just didn't want to let those punks ruin a good Saturday. I looked at the bulky backpack. "What else you got in there?" I asked.

"Got a Nerf football," said Deuce.

A few minutes later, I had it in my hands, ready to air it out.

"Mike, you go long," I said. "And Deuce?"

"I know, I know," he said. "Go short."

We had a good time playing — I got my best grass stain of the day diving for one of Mike's passes. Still, it kind of bothered me that we'd let those guys kick us off our own home court.

CHAPTER 7

I woke up Sunday with stuff to do, and as soon as I hit the kitchen, Dad added one more thing to the list. He was holding up my shorts from yesterday like Exhibit A in the Crime of the Century. I'd just thrown them in with the rest of the laundry. I guess that was wishful thinking.

"Think I can see some cloth in between all these grass stains," he said. Then he leaned in and put his eyes right up close.

"Yeah," I started (what was I going to do, deny it?), "we played some baseball and I was in the outfield, and then there was some Nerf —"

"I don't know about Nerf, but there's definitely some turf," he said, cutting me off. Then he tossed me the shorts. "Those are good shorts, so you get those stains out of there even if you've got to use a washboard."

I grabbed the grungy shorts out of the air and put them back by the washer. I sort of made a mental note to add it to my list of things to avoid doing. I looked around at the detergents and all that stuff. Whatever a washboard was, I didn't think we had one.

Sunday was always kind of heavy on chores. I also had to get some serious work done on that history paper, plus the rest of my homework. I had kind of a panicky feeling when I realized how much that was. That feeling must've passed pretty quickly, though, because I was down at the little park with my skateboard an hour later.

I was rolling along the pavement at the bottom of a set of concrete steps. I tried an ollie and nailed it. Even though it was just a small one, it felt cool to jump through the air with the board stuck right to my sneakers. I felt like Superman, if Superman had any reason to skate.

When I landed, I still had some decent speed. I tried to hop up on the first step for a boardslide. The steps had worn-down metal edges, so they were perfect, but I doinked it. The board got hung up on the edge and I went flying. And this time, it wasn't the Superman kind of flying. I had to catch myself on the railing to avoid feeling like Clark Kent in the worst possible way.

That was okay. It was just my first attempt of the day, and I already knew I could do a boardslide. I was just trying to get a little better at both tricks and to start linking them together. It's just like basketball: Okay, so you can dribble and you can shoot. Now, dribble and shoot. Put those together for a pull-up jumper.

The next trick I wanted to learn was a little tougher. I wanted to have these two down before I tried the pop-shuvit. In that one, you pop the board up in the air so that it's spinning around under you. Then its wheels land on the ground right before you land on it. That was the idea at least. The few times I'd tried it, the wheels had landed somewhere else, and I was the one who ended up on the ground.

Anyway, I worked on those first two tricks for a while, but before too long I had to leave to get back home. I wasn't that late when I rolled into the driveway, but Junior was out there dribbling a basketball. "Come help me out," he said, as if he were painting the house instead of working on his ballhandling.

And what am I going to do, not help my older brother? So we got into it. He'd shield me off with his body; trying to get around him was like trying to get to the other side of a building. My brother definitely had more size to work with. When he'd back me down toward the imaginary basket, there wasn't much I could do. But then he'd help me out by dribbling high or out away from his body, and I'd shoot around for the steal.

"Oh, man, got me again," he'd say. Or, "Where'd you come from?" He pretended he hadn't helped me out at all, but he always had a sneaky little smile on his face.

"Guess I was just lucky," I'd say. In a way, I was: lucky to have an older brother who'd play hoops with me without Mack-trucking me into the pavement. We just had fun. There was no basket, but there were no bullies or sign-up sheets either. We were out there for an hour, even though we both had chores to do. Or maybe *because* we both had chores to do.

"Wash!" Dad called as soon as I walked in the door. I wasn't one hundred percent sure if he meant me or those darn shorts, but I figured I could do both at the same time. I used my dirty hands to carry my dirtier shorts over to

the sink. I knew from years of grass-stain experience — I was practically an expert — that you had to get most of the stain out before you put it in the washer.

"Mmm-hmmm," said Dad when he walked by and saw me bent over the sink and scrubbing away. "That's what I call taking responsibility for your actions."

And that's what I call wrinkly fingers. But fifteen minutes later, the shorts were ready for the washer, and I finally had one chore crossed off my list.

After that, I went to my desk and spread out the stuff for my paper. I'd done the reading, now I had to start writing. My plan was to write three pages. That would leave just one more for tomorrow: the one on what Dr. King meant to me. I couldn't write that tonight anyway. I was still trying to figure it out.

I was getting a little worried about that. If I couldn't come up with something original, and got a bad grade on this big paper, I probably wouldn't make honor roll. That was something Mom and Dad were both pretty proud of, and I didn't want to let them down. Plus, Deuce would be on me for it. I was glad I still had a little time.

Anyway, after spending another day running around

under the sun, it felt kind of good to sit inside the cool, quiet house and flex my brain a little. When the phone rang, I nearly fell out of my seat. I picked it up. "Hello?"

It was Mike: The bullies had kicked him off the court again!

"Yeah," he said. "The other half of the court was basically open, but some random dude showed up and they told me to get lost so they could run full court."

"They told you to get lost?" I asked.

"Yeah, but they didn't put it quite so nicely," he said. "And they've pretty much trashed the court now."

"Think they'll be there again tomorrow?"

"I guarantee it," he said. "Because they told me not to bother coming back."

"Then I guess they'll be pretty surprised," I said.

"You in?" he said.

"Yeah," I said. I knew I might be getting drawn into something big here, and that there were other things I could be doing that were more fun. I'd even heard that Timmy was organizing another baseball game for tomorrow. But I also knew that these were my friends. No one should kick us off our own court, and no one should trash it either. "I'm in."

CHAPTER 8

I had that Game Day feeling all day on Monday.

"So you're sure they'll be there?" Deuce said to Mike as we walked down the hall before math class.

"That's what they said," Mike answered. "And anyway, it sort of seems like they've moved in."

"Seriously," I said. "They've been there every day since the first time."

I wanted to say since the first time we played them, but I hadn't played in that first game. They'd waited until after I left before they agreed to play, just because I was the tallest of our group.

"But they'll play us, right?" I said.

"Yeah, I'm pretty sure," said Mike.

"Yeah," I said, thinking about it. "I guess if they tell you not to come back and you come back with the two of us, they've pretty much got to play."

A thought popped into my head: They have to play, but they don't have to play fair. I didn't say it, though. Nerves were always a big part of that Game Day feeling, and they were an even bigger part today. Everything about the game seemed big, and that definitely included the other team. I remembered what Mike and Deuce looked like limping off the court last time, and I bet they remembered what it felt like.

As soon as we got to our seats for math, Mr. O'Neal began passing out sheets of paper. I knew what was on it before it even landed on my desk: It was a pop quiz. I could just tell by the length of the questions that it was going to be a tough one.

I looked over at my friends. Deuce was on my right, and his pencil was already hovering over the paper, ready to attack the first question. Mike was on my left, holding his forehead in both hands and looking at the questions with wide-open eyes. I looked back down at the quiz. I knew today would be a challenge. I just didn't think it would start so soon.

We headed straight to the court after school. We were hoping to get there first and, you know, establish position. No luck. When we rounded the corner, I could see the older kids were already there.

"What, do these guys live here now or something?" I said.

They were just slinking around and shooting lazy jumpers, so I guess they were still warming up. As we walked toward the court, I saw an iced tea can lying on its side with a sticky brown puddle drying up in front of it. And it had company. More of their junk was scattered around the court and kicked into the corners, with bees and flies buzzing all around it.

Mike and Deuce were both standing up straight with their game faces on, and I did the same. It felt like a war movie, like we were marching into battle.

"This is it," said Deuce.

"Game on," I said.

"Let's do this!" said Mike, a little louder.

We were close enough now, and their biggest guy looked over.

"Well, well, well," he said. "Look who came back for seconds."

I decided right then not to play into their trash talk.

"Three-on-three?" I said, all business.

The older kids looked at each other. They knew it wasn't really a question.

"Be our guests, ladies," said the first guy. "We'll even give you the rock first. But it's make it, take it after that."

"Sure, no problem," I said, ignoring his insult. "What are we playing to?"

"Seven," he said. "Get you three home before your bedtimes."

I looked over at Mike and Deuce to see what they thought. That was a pretty short game. A lot of times we'd play to eleven or even fifteen. And make it, take it — with the team that scores getting the ball back — it could be over in a flash. These guys were probably just trying to get rid of us. On the other hand, it would only take a few good shots and a couple of lucky bounces to get us to seven, no matter how much older they were.

"Sure," said Deuce.

"Whatever the score," said Mike, "we'll get there."

"Funny," said the second-biggest guy. "I don't remember the last game going that way."

Without even really thinking about it, we'd already sort of matched up against the other players. I was standing in front of their tallest guy, and Deuce was matched up against their shortest. Up close like this, you could see they had a height advantage in every matchup.

"What's your name?" I said to my man, Captain Peach Fuzz.

"Carlos," he said, sizing me up for about the fourth time.

"Amar'e."

"Armory?" he said, with a little smirk to show how funny he thought he was.

"A*mar*'e," I said.

"Whatever," he said. "I already forgot it. Let me see your ball."

Deuce bounced it over. It was still pretty new and regulation NBA. Deuce had gotten it for his birthday. As soon as Carlos got his hands on it, just the way he grabbed it, I thought, *I don't know if we're getting that back.*

"We'll use this one," said Carlos. He had long fingers that made the ball look small, and he had dirt under his nails. As soon as the game started, I found out that his nails weren't nearly the dirtiest thing about him.

Deuce took the ball out from the top of the key. His size was a problem when he was shooting, but it worked to his advantage when it came to ballhandling. He stayed low and kept his dribbling under control, even at top speed. It was really hard for anyone to get down there and strip the ball away.

He got around his guy, and I got a little separation from mine. I had an open path to the basket, and Deuce fired a lead pass into the space in front of me. I sprinted forward to grab it out of the air. My eyes were on the ball, so I didn't see Carlos stick out his leg. I sure felt it, though. His shin banged into mine just above my ankle and I tumbled hard onto the pavement. All I could do was watch the ball sail out-of-bounds as I was going down.

"Foul!" I said, climbing to my feet. I had a scraped-up

elbow and a banged-up ankle, and I was lucky it wasn't any worse.

"Nah," said Carlos. "You just tripped. In fact, it was probably an offensive foul on you. But I'll let it slide this time. Our ball."

So that right there gives you an idea of what we were dealing with. I D'd up Carlos, and I wasn't shy about it. He kept going to his left, so I figured out pretty quick that he was left-handed. I got right up on him and played hard, but it wasn't just his fingers that were long. He had long arms and legs. Even his neck was long! When he came at me, it was like some flying collection of elbows and knees. Somewhere in there was the ball.

He scored the first basket of the game on a big, loopy hook shot. The ball came off the tips of his fingers at the top of his outstretched arm. I had good length, too, but watching that release made me feel like I was going to need a ladder to defend him.

I worked hard and managed to stop him on the next drive, but he just passed it off for another bucket. Mike was matched up against a guy they kept calling "Yeti." It was a pretty good nickname for him, too, because this kid was built like a monster. He wasn't more than an inch taller than Mike, but his shoulders and hips were so wide and square that it looked like someone had thrown a T-shirt on a footlocker.

Carlos dropped the ball down to him in the post and Yeti dropped his shoulder into Mike.

"Oooooof!" went Mike. He couldn't help but take a few steps back, and Yeti took advantage of the extra space for an easy layup.

The game had barely started and they were already up 2–0. But they tried the exact same play on the next possession, and Mike saw it coming. He stepped in front of Yeti and deflected the ball straight to Deuce. He dribbled around the perimeter a little, and Mike and I got busy trying to get open.

It wasn't easy, since my defender was long and Mike's was wide. Deuce looked around and decided to take the ball himself. His defender was taller than him, which was no major surprise. They called him Ledge or something that sounded like that. I'm just going to say it: Ledge was one greasy dude. He sweated a lot and when he got sweaty he looked sort of *oily*.

His hands were always moving, too, slapping at the ball, slapping at the air, and sometimes slapping at Deuce. You could see it was bothering him. Would you want some greasy guy slapping at you all game?

"Turn on the jets, D!" I called out.

Deuce gave Ledge that lightning-fast first step and managed to get a little space. I made a move to get in front of Carlos.

"Now!" I raised both hands in front of me, palms up.

But Deuce waited a little too long to make the pass. Ledge recovered and slapped the ball loose. I have to admit, he really did move fast. Must've been all that grease. The bullies scored two more points before we got the ball back. When we did, I posted up near the basket and got us on the board with a skyhook of my own.

"Lucky," said Carlos as the ball rattled in.

"You think you're the only one who's ever hit a hook shot?" I said.

There was a little bricklaying by both teams after that, but we managed to get three more points down the stretch. We got it to 6–4, but they kept playing dirty the whole time.

On one play, Yeti clobbered Deuce on a moving pick. It was the biggest player on the court taking out the smallest, and it was hard to miss the foul. But mostly they were trickier than that. They specialized in border-line fouls, things that a real ref would've called, but that weren't obvious enough to get out here on the play-ground. It really got to us after a while.

"Get off me, man," Deuce said as Ledge pawed and slapped away.

He passed the ball off to Mike, who had pretty good position to the right of the basket. But as soon as Mike got it, Yeti started grinding his forearm and elbow into Mike's back.

"Over here!" I called, because I could see he wasn't going to be able to back in any closer.

Mike fired the ball to me as I flashed into the open. I tried to swing wide as I came around to the left side of the basket. I had to keep an eye out for Carlos's long arms, so he couldn't reach in and grab the ball, and I had to keep an eye on his long legs, so he couldn't trip me again. I guess I just ran out of eyes because I tripped on a crack in the pavement.

The worst thing about it was that I *knew* there was a big crack there on the left side. Carlos had been going to that side all game because he was a lefty. I'd just gotten so distracted by all of his cheap shots and hacks that I'd forgotten about it.

I didn't go down, but it didn't matter. I stumbled and lost control of the ball. Carlos shot forward and took possession. He threw a quick pass back to Ledge at the free throw line. Ledge launched a laser to Yeti under the basket, and he knocked into Mike on his way to another layup. That was it, game over, 7–4.

Being a sore loser is one thing, but being a bad winner? That's just low.

"Never in doubt," said Carlos, acting like he'd already forgotten the points I scored against him.

Yeti pulled a can of soda out of his bag. "Too easy," he said, in between long gulps.

Ledge was licking his lips like a frog and watching Yeti guzzle his warm soda.

The only good thing was we got Deuce's good ball back. I jumped up and grabbed it as it came through the hoop. It felt weird to rebound a ball that had already gone in, but I knew it was the only way we'd get it back.

"At least this one was close," said Deuce.

"How many points did you guys score last time?" I said.

"Two," said Mike.

I'd scored two points myself this time, and Mike and Deuce had one apiece. But it was hard to feel good about the improvement when the rest of us felt so bad.

"Ow, my back," said Mike as we headed off the court. "I'm going to be feeling those elbows all week!"

"For real," said Deuce. "I think I need about four showers to get that guy's slime off me!"

I looked down at my own scrapes and bruises.

"What's that on your arm there?" said Mike, pointing.

"Scratches," I said. Just looking at them gave me a queasy feeling.

"You mean . . . ?" said Deuce.

"Yeah," I said. "Even his fingernails were long."

We were off the court and on the little path that led to the road when we heard Yeti call out behind us: "Hey, losers!"

I turned around, even though I knew this wasn't going to be anything good. Yeti had finished his soda and was holding the empty can. As I watched, he twisted it so the metal bent in the middle. Then he smashed it flat between his big meaty hands.

"Catch!" yelled Yeti, and tossed it at us.

I watched the metal disk fly through the air and sail just off to our left. I'd seen a can just like that on Saturday. That's when I knew: These were the guys who'd been making my dad's job harder.

CHAPTER 9

I was in a pretty bad mood by the time I made it home. I just wanted to head inside and maybe zone out with some TV. But when I got there, Dad was pulling up from the other direction. The big trailer bounced up and over the curb as it made the wide, slow turn into the driveway. I walked alongside the truck as it eased to a stop. Then I waited for Dad to get out.

"Now that was a full day's work," he said, as he stepped down out of the driver's seat. He swung the door shut behind him, and turned toward me. He was about to say something else, but as soon as he got a good look at me, he stopped.

"Hey, Pops," I said.

I could see his eyes taking in my scraped-up knee and my scratched-up arm. He was looking at me the way I once saw a guy look at his car after a fender bender downtown, carefully sizing up the damage. The only difference was that my dad wasn't thinking about the repair costs. He was probably just wondering what had happened to his kid.

"You look worse than I do," he said, "and I've been using a wood chipper all day!"

He was trying to cheer me up. I tried to smile, but I couldn't get the corners of my mouth to move any way but down.

"I knew it was a mistake to play," I said.

"What do you mean, STAT?" he said.

Like I said before, STAT stood for Standing Tall And Talented. I usually liked that, but I wasn't feeling all that Tall or Talented at the moment.

"I should've just gone skateboarding or played baseball with Timmy and them," I said. The words came out in one big blurt.

"You didn't get those scratches from a hardball," said Dad.

"I was playing hoops with Mike and Deuce," I said.

"Nothing wrong with playing ball with your boys," said Dad.

"No, I know, it's just . . ." I was trying to think of how to explain. "There are these kids who've been hogging the court. And I knew if I got dragged into it, it would end up being this whole big thing."

I stopped and ran that back to see if it made any sense or if Dad was going to say anything about it. He was still standing there, though. He was wiping his hands on his work pants, but his eyes were still looking at mine. He was still listening to what I had to say. He knew before I did that there was more coming.

"Those guys are my best friends," I said. "It's just that they always want me to be playing hoops with them, but I'm into a bunch of things."

"Yeah," said my dad. "You sure don't have any trouble keeping yourself busy."

"I like baseball, football, skateboarding, and even reading about history and stuff," I said. I didn't even mention the music, movies, bowling, and other things. This was my dad, and he knew me as well as anyone. That's how he knew that it was his turn to talk.

He put his big hands on his hips and looked back at the truck. Maybe he was checking something and maybe he was just putting his words in order. I think it might have been that second thing, because when he started talking, he seemed to know just what to say.

"Son, we both know that you've got a gift for basketball," he said. "But your greatest gift is just being you. And like you said, that includes a lot of different interests. What you have to understand is that it's not one or the other. You can play hoops with your friends and still be yourself."

"I guess," I said.

He looked back at the trailer again, and this time he pointed to it. "It's just like you're part of my crew when you work, but you have your own thing," he said. "Those big riding mowers can't trim around those little trees and flower bushes. They'd run 'em right over. But you've never so much as plucked a petal."

I thought about all the times I wheeled that little lawn mower around. All the birdbaths and rose bushes I'd ducked and dodged.

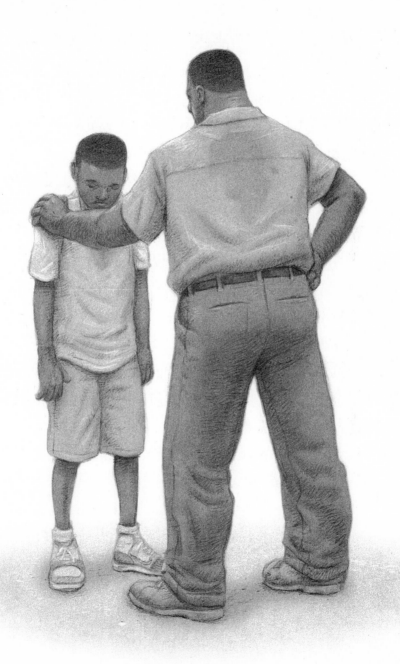

"Basketball's like that," he said. "You find your own thing out there, and your friends find theirs." He reached over and put his hand on my shoulder. "But I'll tell you one thing, son. When you find your place out there, you won't be any little push mower on the court."

We stood there on the lawn, and I felt those last words sink in. I appreciated it, but talking about that mower reminded me I had something else to say.

"I think this is the same group that's been messing up all your lawns," I said. "They just started coming around here, and they made the same kind of mess on the court."

I thought Dad would be really mad, but he just shook his head. "Listen, STAT," he said. "I've been around a long time, and I've dealt with a lot worse than those kids. Don't you worry about that. I can take care of the lawns. You just take care of what you need to."

Right then, I knew what I had to do. My dad could take care of his turf. Now I needed to take care of mine. That smile, the one I was trying to make before, came out on its own now.

"Thanks, Dad," I said.

After dinner, I thought about what he'd said for a long time. Later that night, I made some phone calls. I got through to Deuce first.

"Yo, D," I said.

"'Sup, man?" he said.

I got right to the point: "We're playing them again tomorrow."

He didn't say anything at first. Finally he said, "You sure?"

I was.

"Trust me," I said. "I have a plan."

"Oh, yeah?"

"Yeah."

He wanted to know what it was, but I couldn't tell him just yet. I was still working out the details.

"But you'll be there, right?" I said.

"Amar'e, man, it's me," he said. "You know I will."

"Yeah," I said. "I know it."

Even before I made the next call, I knew Mike would be there, too. We all would.

CHAPTER 10

*T*uesday started out like a time warp. It was Game Day — again! I had some of the same nerves. And a few times I wondered what I'd gotten myself — and my friends — into. But mostly I was too busy to think about that situation. I got started first thing.

"Yo, Marcus!" I said.

"What's up, Amar'e?" he said.

English class was about to start. It was our first class of the day, and while Marcus was waiting for my answer, his mouth opened in a big, round yawn.

"Sorry, man," he said. "Still sleepy."

"No problem," I said. "I'm going to let you in on

something. And it isn't until after school, so you'll have plenty of time to wake up for it."

Marcus liked to be in the know. If you wanted to get his attention, all you had to do was act like whatever you were telling him was a secret. His eyes blinked open a little wider, and he leaned a little closer across the aisle between our desks.

"Yeah?" he said. "What is it?"

"There's gonna be a big game over at the basketball court on Sycamore," I said. "You know the one?"

"Yeah," he said. "It's near my bus stop."

"Okay, cool," I said. Then I looked around, acting like I was double-checking that no one else was listening. "Mike, Deuce, and I are taking on some older kids: real nasty ones."

Marcus looked around, too.

"Yeah?" he whispered.

"Yeah," I said. "High stakes, too. Like, sky-high."

He was about to ask what was on the line to make the stakes so high, but the bell cut him off. We leaned back into our seats as class got started. The ball was rolling now. There were two things about Marcus. The first one I already told you: He liked secrets. The second one: He never could keep them. By third period, all his other friends would know. By fifth, most of their friends probably would, too.

There was no sense getting lazy, though, so I kept at it. I told a lot of kids, especially ones who I knew were into basketball. Timmy was a year older and a grade ahead, but I caught sight of him between classes and sprinted to catch up.

"I'll be there, big man," he said, giving me a fist bump.

I ran into Janie before our next class. She was a really good player herself, but that's not why I absolutely had to tell her about the game. Deuce had "kind of a thing" for her. He'd admitted that once to Mike and me. He's denied it ever since, but that was like trying to get toothpaste back in the tube. I knew that having her there would guarantee he played his best.

By the time I caught up with Tavoris in gym, he already knew all about it.

"Marcus tell you?" I asked.

"Mouth of the south," said Tavoris, smiling.

I smiled, too. I was glad so many people knew already, and glad that an older kid like Timmy would be there. The way I saw it, with so many eyes on them, even Carlos and his crew of bruisers couldn't get too out of hand. We'd only lost by three points, and just playing a fair game seemed like it might be worth a point or two. As for the other point or two we'd need, I had an idea where that might come from.

By lunchtime, people were talking about the game. There were even some crazy rumors going around.

"Did you hear?" said Deuce, sliding his tray onto the table next to mine. "They're saying one of the kids is six foot five!"

"And another one is as hairy as a bigfoot!" said Mike.

We'd all been doing our part to spread the word. Now we were doing what my dad called sitting back and enjoying the fruits of our labor.

"There are going to be a ton of kids there," said Deuce.

"Good," I said. "That's the plan."

"Yeah," said Mike. "But it's only good *if we win.*"

He was right. We were taking a big risk.

"I admit it," I said, shrugging. "The second part of the plan is a little tougher."

"I just hope we don't end up looking like punks in front of half the class," said Deuce.

It was a serious point, and I would have given him a serious answer. But that was when the mixed vegetables started flying. If they were ever real vegetables, it was a long time ago. By the time they were dropped onto our lunch trays, they were slimy and a little too gray to really eat. A lot of kids thought they were just right for flinging though.

"Yo, Mike," I said, pointing to the top of his head. "String bean."

He plucked it out of his hair. It looked like a greenish-grayish slug. As he pinched it between his fingers, some kind of liquid came burbling out of the end.

"Nasty!" he said.

Then he turned around. Maybe he threw it back at the kid who'd pegged him with it. Maybe he got him right on the cheek. You won't hear it from me, though. Unlike Marcus, I can keep a secret.

After lunch, the nerves really started to set in. Getting a big crowd there might help us win, but it would also make it much worse if we lost. On our way to history, we walked right by the sign-up sheet for the tournament. I'd sort of forgotten about it with all of this game drama going on. I took a quick look as we passed by: just a few spots left.

I hadn't forgotten about history, though. We ducked into class just in time. I ran my hands through my hair, just to confirm that there were no vegetable slugs up there, then I opened my notebook. I'd finished writing most of the paper last night.

But I still wasn't sure exactly what Dr. King meant to me. I knew what he meant to civil rights and to America and all the big things — it said that part right in the book — but I still couldn't put that last part into words. And the paper was due *tomorrow*. Time flies when you don't know the answer.

I took one look at Ms. Bourne standing at the front of the room with a serious look on her face, and I knew copying that same answer out of the book wasn't going to cut it. On the plus side, at least worrying about that took my mind off the game for a while.

But that class ended, and so did the one after that. All I had to do next was this: play the game of my life, and hope my friends did, too!

CHAPTER 11

There was already a crowd at the court by the time we arrived. And Carlos's crew was right at the center of it, hogging the good side of the court as usual. Yeti was hanging on the rim again like a jerk.

"He's going to bend that one, too," I said.

"He might bend us," said Mike.

"You want me to guard him today?" I asked.

"Nah," said Mike. "I'm not tall enough to take Carlos. I'm just not looking forward to those elbows is all."

"This'll be the last time you have to deal with them," I said. "One way or the other."

"Wanna bet?" said Mike.

"That's exactly what I intend to do," I said.

"Huh?" said Mike and Deuce at the same time.

By now, some of the kids from our class had seen us.

"Here they come!" called Janie.

"It's on!" shouted Tavoris.

Carlos and his buddies turned to see what was going on. Once they saw it was us, you could tell they weren't all that impressed.

"What are you guys doing back on our court?" said Carlos the moment we stepped onto it.

"Shouldn't you be home with your tails between your legs?" said Ledge.

"Shouldn't you go back to the garbage dump you came from?" I said, kicking one of Yeti's flattened cans across the court toward them. My heart was pounding like a jackhammer. Was it possible these three had gotten even bigger overnight? The can skittered to a stop in front of Carlos. He looked down at it and then back up at me. Then he burst out laughing.

"Man, you have lost it, A*mar*'e," he said. "Who cares about this little court?"

"I don't just mean the court," I said. "You've been leaving your junk all over town."

"So what if we have?" said Carlos. "Let the garbage man deal with it."

That got me heated up. "My dad is not a garbage man!" I said. It must have been loud enough for everyone to hear because the crowd started making noise all around us.

"Oh, now we're getting somewhere," said Carlos, clapping his long hands together. "You hear that, guys? This kid's dad is the garbage man, been picking up after us!"

"Like father, like son," said Ledge. He let out a wheezy little laugh and Yeti low-fived him.

"He owns a lawn-care comp —" I started, but there was no point. These three had no class to begin with, so why would they start now? I just needed to put my plan in action. I wasn't one hundred percent sure about what came next, but I didn't let it show in my voice. I raised my head, and said loud and clear: "We decided to come back and take out the trash ourselves. And guess who's the trash?"

A chorus of ooooooh's went through the kids ringing the court.

Carlos looked around at the audience, and I saw his eyes stop somewhere back over my shoulder. I turned around and saw Junior walking up from the street with Timmy. He wasn't part of the plan, but I was definitely glad to see my older bro.

"What are you doing here, man?" I asked.

"Heard there was a big game going on," he said with a little shrug and a big smile.

"There is," I said. Then I turned back to Carlos.

"So what, you've got some friends," he said. "Doesn't change a thing. We'll still crush you."

I looked right at him and said: "Wanna bet?"

Another round of ooooooh's rippled through the crowd. Carlos looked around. He was definitely annoyed. "What do you have in mind?" he said.

I waited a few seconds until the court was quiet. I wanted everyone to hear this. "Make it, take it," I said.

"Sure," said Carlos.

"I mean the court," I said.

"Huh?" he said.

"What's this kid talking about?" said Yeti, who was standing next to Carlos.

"I mean whoever wins gets the court," I said. "Loser clears out for good!"

"Whoa, whoa, whoa," I heard, but it wasn't from Carlos's side. It was my own team. Deuce and Mike pulled me aside.

"One sec," said Mike, holding up his hands.

They both leaned in and whispered.

"Are you crazy?" said Deuce. "This is our court. We've been playing here since forever. These guys are just, like, visitors. We can wait them out!"

"Yeah," said Mike. "Aren't you on the honor roll?"

I thought about that big history paper. "For now," I said.

"Well, aren't honor roll students supposed to be smart?" he said. "You're risking our home court."

"Hey!" said Deuce. "I'm on the honor roll, too, and I think this is stone-cold crazy."

"Come on," I said. "We've already lost this court. We have to check every day to see if these guys are here. And we'd have to do that every day for, like, ever. We couldn't ever just come up here for a game without worrying about it. Plus, they haven't missed a day since they showed up. Let's face it — they think this is their court now."

Mike and Deuce looked at each other.

"Yeah," said Mike. "You've got a point."

"I guess," said Deuce.

"Trust me," I said.

They looked up at all the kids from school and then looked back at me.

"Okay," said Mike.

Deuce just nodded his head yes.

"One other thing," I said, just before I broke from our huddle. "We all need to play the best game of our lives."

"That's just great," said Deuce.

"No pressure there," said Mike.

When I turned around, I saw Carlos breaking from his own huddle. They must've been talking it over, too.

"So?" I said. "Is it a deal, one game for the court?"

"Yeah," said Carlos. "All right."

I reached out my hand. He just looked at it for a few seconds.

"Unless you're afraid," I said, which was pretty funny considering they could probably hear my heart pounding in Georgia.

"Not even a little," said Carlos, reaching out and grabbing my hand. He shook it once, hard. Just like that, it was official.

"To seven again?" I said.

"Yeah," he said. "Let's get this over with fast, so I can start enjoying my new court."

"Win by two?" I said.

"Nope," he said. "First team to seven wins, simple as that."

Man, I thought. *He sounds really confident, even with all these eyes on him.*

"First team to seven!" Marcus called out, in case anyone in the back hadn't heard.

There was no backing out now. There were only two ways to leave this court now: as winners or forever.

CHAPTER 12

We were down 0–1 faster than I could say "Uh-oh." The other team ran a slick pick-and-roll that forced us to switch up our defense in the middle of the play. Deuce wound up on Yeti, who was too big for him, and Mike wound up on Ledge, who was too quick. They practically had their choice of how to score, so of course they chose option (C) None of the above.

As soon as the ball went to Yeti, I left Carlos to try to help Deuce out. And as soon as I did that, Yeti threw it back to Carlos, who was already sprinting to the hoop. He launched himself up toward the rim and dunked it. It wasn't exactly a tomahawk jam. If his fingers hadn't been so long, he might not have gotten it through at all. But it didn't matter: They schooled us in about three different ways on the play and finished it with a dunk.

Now the ooooooh's going through the crowd were for them. Kids were standing around the edge of the court, sitting on the grass, or hanging from the fence. Some of them were our friends, but some of them I barely knew.

"Not good," I said to my teammates.

"Hold up," I heard. It was Junior. "Huddle up for a second, guys."

"Who are you?" barked Carlos.

"I'm their coach!" said Junior. I guess that was good enough for Carlos — that and Junior's size — because he didn't say another word about it.

"Now I remember where I've seen these guys," my coach/brother said to us. "They're part of a travel team from the next town over. I've seen 'em play. That's why they were so smooth on that pick-and-roll. So listen up: You've got to work through that pick, and you can't double switch like that."

We listened as he broke it down for us. I clapped my hands hard as we left the huddle. Then Deuce checked the ball back to Ledge for their next possession.

"We need a stop!" said Mike, and he got us one the hard way. Yeti ran over him on the way to the hoop. Mike had position and he didn't move his feet at all, not so much as tapping a toe. It was an offensive foul on Yeti, a charge all the way. But that didn't mean we were going to get the call. They hadn't given us any the last game.

"That was a foul!" said Mike, swiping dirt and pebbles off his backside as he got to his feet.

"Nah, nah, nah," Carlos said. "Your feet were —"

A booming voice cut him off: "That was a foul, man!"

I didn't even have to turn to know those words came from the big, barrel chest of my older bro. Then I heard another strong voice chime in from the crowd. "That was a charge all the way!" called Timmy.

Carlos got a look on his face like he'd just whiffed someone's sweaty socks, but he said, "Yeah, okay. I guess we'll give you that one."

Deuce and I high-fived Mike. "Nice play," I said.

"Thanks," he said. "But I don't know how many more of those I can take."

Our first possession wasn't half as precise as theirs. We passed it around the perimeter a few times to get in the flow of things. Finally, on the third pass, one of them got lazy. Ledge was sort of laying off Deuce, so I put something extra on my pass. It was a bullet, and Ledge was still out of position when Deuce caught it. That gave our fastest player the half step he needed. He turned on the jets and beat everyone to the hoop. He laid it up to tie the score.

We felt good about that. Deuce smiled and even risked a quick *how ya like me now* look over at Janie, just to make sure she'd seen the play. That all lasted for about 0.5 seconds.

Deuce tried to return the favor on our next possession, but Carlos saw the long lead pass coming and picked it off. Then they went to work down low. Yeti scored on two straight possessions. He didn't run over Mike. He just backed into him, leaning on him with his big body. Yeti was wearing an old white T-shirt, so it sort of looked like Mike was trying to defend against a refrigerator.

Just like that, they were up 3–1. It looked like that refrigerator might put us on ice. Junior huddled us up before the next possession. "Come on, guys," he said.

"That big dude is killing us," said Deuce.

"You're telling me," said Mike. "And I thought I was sore *before* the game!"

"Any ideas?" said Deuce. He was looking at our coach, but all my bro came up with was: "Don't suppose Mike could put on twenty pounds in the next few minutes?"

It wasn't exactly textbook coaching, but least it loosened us up a little.

"I've got an idea," I said. "Let's all collapse down next time he gets it. His body is big, but his handle looks kinda shaky."

I wasn't sure it would work, but we didn't have to wait long to find out. They dumped the ball down to Yeti as soon as they got it. And when the ball went into the post, we did, too. Deuce and I both dropped down. Ledge and Carlos didn't understand why we were giving up position, but they were happy to follow us closer to the basket. Both of them had their hands up, but Yeti had his head down, as usual.

He had Mike blocked off with his body and was dribbling the ball in big, lazy bounces. It was practically at head level for Deuce, who reached in for an easy steal. Now I was the one with my hands up. Deuce hit me with

a sweet no-look pass, and I went right up with it. I heard one of Carlos's fingernails tick off the leather, but it wasn't enough. The ball went in, and Carlos came down shaking his hand.

It was 3–2, and now our friends in the crowd had something to cheer about.

We traded a few bricks after that, with both teams missing long jump shots. Then we traded buckets, making it 4–3. We were right in the game and feeling pretty good, but when we traded baskets again, I started to worry.

I'd just answered another one of Carlos's patented hook shots with a little up-and-under move. Now it was 5–4. Our classmates were enjoying the close game, but if we didn't close the gap, we were going to lose.

Even worse, we were getting worn down. They weren't fouling us as much as last game, but they were bigger at every position and playing hard. It was taking a toll. Deuce's jets were running out of fuel, and Mike was wincing every time Yeti so much as touched his back.

Sure enough, it came back to bite us. Deuce dumped the ball down to Mike. He had good position, no more than three or four feet from the hoop. But Yeti jammed his elbow hard into his lower back. Mike grimaced in pain and lost his dribble. Ledge got to the loose ball first and laid it in.

They had a 6–4 lead.

"Game point!" someone called out.

We were dog tired and down by two. It was time to put the second part of my plan into action. It was now or never.

CHAPTER 13

"*H*uddle up, guys!" called Junior.

The other team huddled up, too, and I had a pretty good idea what they were talking about.

"You all know where the ball is going," said Junior.

"Straight to Carlos," I said.

"No doubt about it," agreed Deuce.

Carlos had mostly been happy to spread the ball around so far, dumping it into the post to let Yeti do the dirty work or dropping it back to Ledge for a jumper. But this was game point, and he was definitely the kind of guy who'd want to keep the glory for himself.

"Should we front him?" asked Mike. "Keep him from getting the ball?"

"Or maybe we should double-team him as soon as he gets it?" said Deuce.

"I've got a better idea," I said.

They leaned in a little closer to hear it.

"Let him have it," I said.

"You sure?" said Junior.

"Yeah," I said, looking right at him. He nodded. Coach or not, he knew me well enough to know when I had something up my sleeve.

Mike hadn't known me quite as long. He looked confused for a second. "Wait," he said. "You mean really let him have it." He punched his left palm with his right fist to show what he meant.

"Nah, nah," I said, letting out a little laugh. "Man, you are one brave dude, though. I mean let him have the ball."

"But he's their best player," said Deuce.

"And you know he'll take the shot," said Mike. "Your D is tight, man. But he's got those crazy-long arms, and if he makes it, it's over."

"Yeah, but he likes to go left, right?" I said. I probably could've put that better, but they knew what I meant.

Ten feet away, the other huddle had broken up.

"Talking time is over, losers," I heard Carlos call out.

"So I'm gonna let him go left," I said, hurrying to finish.

"Unless y'all are making out in there!" called Ledge.

Some of the kids in the crowd laughed. That's how it was: Some of them would like whoever won. They were just warming up their butt-kissing muscles.

"He's gonna go left," I said in a fast whisper. "Just be ready when he gets near the sideline."

Junior shot a quick look over at the left sideline and smiled.

"All right," said Deuce. His last words before we broke out of the huddle: "I hope you know what you're doing."

"Me too," I said. It didn't matter if the other team heard that part.

"Check the ball, suckers," said Ledge. He was doing that froggy lip-licking thing again.

Deuce checked it back to him. Two seconds later, it was on its way to Carlos. He reached up with his long, thin fingers and plucked it out of the air like it was a softball. Now it was just me and him, one-on-one. I swallowed hard.

"Come on, 'mar'e!" I heard Junior shout.

That made me feel a little better. Even if we lost, even if Carlos blew right by me and jammed it home, I still had my family. I still had friends. It was a nice thought, but I didn't plan on losing.

I got low in a good defensive stance, but I sort of came up on him a little sideways. My left side was a little closer to him, and my left arm was stretched out so that it was almost touching his right hand. That didn't matter because he was dribbling with his left, as usual. I was giving him a little more space over there, and my arm was down on that side.

He sort of cocked his head and looked at me, like a pet dog does when it hears a funny noise. He knew something wasn't quite right about this, but he didn't spend too much time thinking about it. Fact: If you give a guy an open path on his strong side, he is going to take it. Especially if it's game point.

His first step was fast, almost faster than I could handle. I shuffled my feet and managed to stay between him and the basket. He was going full speed now. I was letting him go up the court but forcing him farther out to his left. At first, he was keeping one eye on the ground, like you have to on these cracked outdoor courts. But as he got closer to the sideline, he started shooting those quick looks up instead of down. He was looking at the hoop.

We were getting close to the corner now. You know the spot. NBA players take tons of threes from there because it's a shorter shot and a straight, squared-up look. And that means that we all practice from there all the time, too, heaving it up and trying to do what they do. Even his dribbling changed a little. You know how it does that when someone's about to take a shot? It was going to be one jump shot from the corner. I didn't think I could get up and contest it with his length, and there was a good chance it would go in.

But that's right where the big crack in the court was. It was the one I stumbled over in our last game. That's the whole reason I remembered it. Maybe if Carlos had tripped over it then, he would've remembered it, too. But he hadn't, so he had to learn that lesson now. With his eyes already radar-locked, sizing up the rim, he had no idea it was coming.

"Look out, man," I heard Yeti yell behind me, but it was too late.

The edge of Carlos's sneaker clipped the raised edge of the cracked blacktop.

"What the —?" he blurted.

I didn't answer, just reached in and grabbed the ball as he tumbled sideways toward the fence. I turned fast, and for this weird moment, there were four sets of eyes staring right at me. Yeti and Ledge were facing forward, waiting to rebound in case Carlos missed. And Mike and Deuce were facing me, wanting to be ready for whatever it was I was planning. Now they knew what it was. They stepped in front of their guys, and I had clear sailing to the hoop.

One dribble, two dribbles, pull up, pop! If the rim still had any net left on it, it would've swished. Now it was 6–5. We were still down by one, but we got the ball back.

"You got lucky with this broke-down court," said Carlos.

"And you got played," I said.

He gave me an ice-cold look. One of their empty

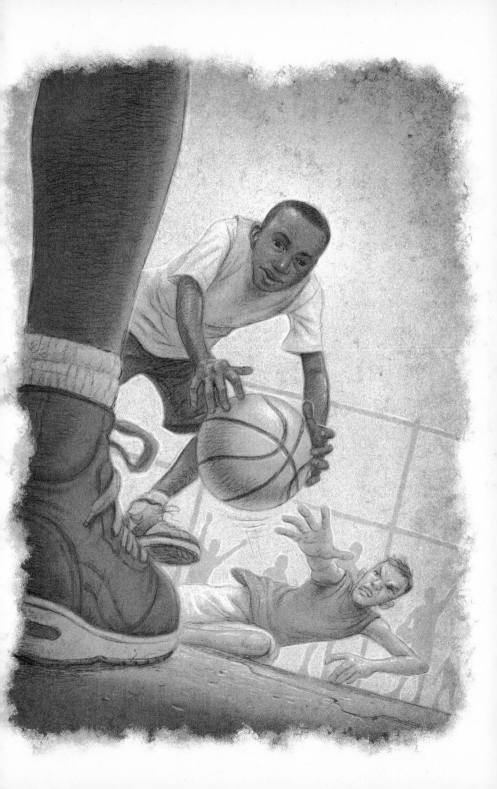

bottles was wedged against the fence. He bent down and picked it up, then tossed it over the fence and out onto the grass. "Better call your dad," he said.

We stared hard at each other. He wanted to get under my skin, and that line definitely got him there. I knew I could expect some tough D this time around. I also knew that same trick wouldn't work again. As it turned out, Deuce had one of his own.

"We need to tie this," he said as Junior huddled us up for the next possession. "Let's fake 'em out."

"How?" said Mike.

I was happy to let those two talk it out with Junior while I leaned over with my hands on my knees and got some oxygen back in my lungs.

"Pretend you're hurt," Deuce whispered to Mike.

"I am hurt!" said Mike, pointing toward his elbow-bashed lower back.

"Right," said Deuce. "Then this should be easy for you!"

"Oh, I get it," I said, raising my head up. "Like playing possum."

The light came on in Mike's eyes. He got it, too. "I'm

really hurting, guys," he said. And this time, he said it loud enough for the other team to "overhear" it.

The next play happened fast.

Ledge checked the ball in to Deuce.

Deuce passed the ball to me, and Carlos was on top of me in a second. There was about an inch between us, and he was slapping away at the ball, shouting in my ear, and generally being a pain in the neck. I moved the ball up the court slowly, shielding Carlos off with my body as best I could.

I was getting closer to Mike and Yeti. But once Yeti saw how Mike was holding his back and almost doubled over, he started shading over to double-team me. Now I had even less space!

Of course, I didn't need much to loop a short pass over Yeti. Mike dropped the act and burst into the open. It caught everyone by surprise, not just the other team, but the crowd, too. No one had been surprised to see Mike hurting after absorbing all of those elbows, but they were all surprised now. Surprised and, in Yeti's case, out of position.

Mike laid it up to tie the score at 6–6.

"Game point," called Tavoris. "For our guys!"

There were some cheers up and down the sidelines. Deuce, Mike, and I high-fived on our way back up court. But that was it: We were fresh out of trick plays, and it was game point for the other team, too. From the looks on their faces, I could tell this game was going to have a rough ending, one way or the other.

Junior huddled us up one last time, and this time, he kept it quick.

"This is going to come down to one play," he said. "Let's make it your best."

He looked right at me. "You know what I'm talking about."

I did. "Pick-and-roll," I said.

Carlos had scored the first point of the game with it, and I planned to score the last. It was my best play. I'd run it a thousand times with these same guys on this same court. I'd even worked on it a few times in the driveway with Junior and my dad — talk about two guys who could set a screen! Now I just needed to run it once, but it had to be perfect.

I looked around at my friends. We were somewhere between beat-down and beat-up. We were one point away from winning, and we were one point away from losing and being kicked off our own court for good. But none of us were backing down. We all clapped once, hard, as we broke the huddle.

"Let's go!" said Mike.

"One more," said Deuce as he walked past me to take the ball out up top. We made eye contact, and he gave me a little nod. I nodded back. We were both ready. Carlos stepped in front of me and got into position. He looked like a boxer before the bell. He was ready, too.

CHAPTER 14

Bomp Bomp Bomp! I heard. *Bomp Bomp Bomp!*

It was either my heart beating out of my chest or Deuce had started dribbling. I admit I was a little nervous. We had this one shot to win the game, but a turnover or a miss, and the other team could win in a second. They were bigger and less beat-up. We had this one chance, and we definitely couldn't count on getting another one. So I got to work.

Carlos was right up on me, and that was fine because that's exactly where I wanted him. Deuce doubled back and started dribbling toward us. The sound of the ball got louder as he got closer. *Bomp BoMP BOMP!* went the ball on the blacktop.

Deuce wasn't moving all that fast. And since he was moving side to side, and not toward the basket, Ledge wasn't on him all that tight. It was like the whole game was in slow motion, but I knew all that was about to change. I took one last look around, just to make sure I knew exactly where I was on the court, and where everyone else was, too.

Our classmates were climbing the fence. I don't mean that like a figure of speech: They were really climbing the chain-link fence behind the hoop. Everyone wanted a good look at game point, no matter who scored it. Tavoris was looking right at me from a spot almost as high as the basket. The wire of the fence made it look like he was wearing crazy, lopsided glasses. I looked over at Mike in the post, with Yeti all over him like an avalanche.

Deuce was getting closer now. The possibility of a pick-and-roll had probably already occurred to Carlos and Ledge. As part of a travel team, they must've practiced it all the time. Carlos was still on me like plastic wrap.

I looked at Deuce and he looked at me. I don't know if it was ESP or ESPN, but I saw it in his eyes: He was ready to go — and he was going to go fast!

Deuce turned on the afterburners. Carlos and Ledge may have been ready for the pick-and-roll, but speed like that changes everything. They didn't have as much time as they thought they would, and that changed the space, too. Deuce was almost even with me now. Ledge had been laying off him a little, and Carlos had been right up on me. And that put them on a collision course.

I stood up straight and held my position as Deuce rocketed past me with the ball.

"Watch it, man!" Carlos shouted as Ledge rushed to keep up. Their legs tangled up as Ledge tried to slip by on the outside. That was my cue. I rolled back away from Carlos. As he pushed his own teammate out of his way, I took off toward the basket.

Deuce was in the clear, and he turned and fired a bounce pass my way. It was a good one, but Carlos had almost as much bounce as the ball did. By the time I got possession, he'd brushed past Ledge and was just a half step behind me.

We raced toward the hoop.

Yeti stepped in front of me. He was too wide to go around.

Carlos was right behind me. If I went up for a shot now, he'd block it from behind.

I gave a quick shot fake — and then ducked!

Carlos went flying over me, swiping at where the ball had been. He came down with a crash — right on Yeti. The two big dudes turned into a tangled mess on the court.

"Take it!" yelled Mike.

It was game point, but I tried not to think about that. Instead, I thought about all the times I'd hit this same shot from this same spot on this same court. I rose up and drained a six-foot jump shot to win the game.

Before my sneakers even landed, shouts went up all around the court. Tavoris raised his hands in triumph. Unfortunately, he'd been using those hands to hold himself on the fence. He thumped into the grass, but he was still smiling. I was, too.

Mike and Deuce ran over, but we were too excited to figure out whether to high-five or fist-bump or what. We just sort of smashed into each other and shouted, "Yeah!"

"Nice shot!" Junior said as he stepped out onto the court.

"Way to go, cuz," Timmy shouted to Deuce. "Clutch shot, big man!" he said to me.

Mike grabbed his back and yelled, "Medic!" Everyone laughed. We all felt too good to really feel the bumps and bruises right now.

Then the court got quiet again and a long shadow fell over me. Carlos had gotten back up and was coming right toward me. Yeti and Ledge were behind him.

"Got your back, Amar'e," Junior said under his breath.

But when Carlos reached me, he wasn't making a fist. He had his hand out. Remember what I said about not being a bad winner? I meant it. I took his hand and shook it.

"Good game, Amar'e," he said, but the look on his face was like he was plucking out a splinter.

"Call me STAT," I said.

And it was true: Mike, Deuce, and I had all stood tall today.

Carlos and his crew slinked off the court and headed for the road. The rest of us got back to enjoying our home-court advantage. Kids from school were joking around, shooting lazy jumpers, and having a good time.

Mike was over in the corner, showing Marcus and some of the other guys exactly how he'd fooled Yeti on that play. He was playing both parts and adding funny faces. When he played Yeti, he put on a confused expression and walked around with his knuckles dragging like a caveman.

Deuce was making a pretty funny expression, too, but his wasn't on purpose. He was talking to Janie and trying to look all cool. I don't know what he was saying, but I saw him wave his hand a few times, like *Aww, it was nothing.*

It wasn't, though. It was something. This whole game was something.

It took us a solid ten minutes to realize the bullies had walked off with the good basketball.

CHAPTER 15

I walked home with my brother, or, I don't know, maybe I kind of floated.

"This trip is quicker on a skateboard," I said.

"Look at me, man," he said. "I'd break a skateboard."

"Yeah, I'm getting a little tall for it, too," I said.

It made me think of that first game against the bullies, the one where they'd waited until I went down to the road to skate before they agreed to play. I told my brother the story. When I finished, he nodded.

"I know those kids," he said.

"You know Carlos?" I asked.

"I know his reputation," he said, "and I know his type, too."

I knew what he meant. "Well, why do they have to be such . . . ?"

"What?" said my brother. "Jerks? Bullies? Who knows? There are probably as many reasons as there are kids like that. I'll tell you one thing I've noticed. Some people get kicked around, and they look for someplace to hide. Some people get kicked around, and they look for someone they can kick."

"Yeah," I said. "I guess."

But I knew he was right. He was five years older than me, and he'd been out there in the world a lot more than me. He'd seen a lot more, including some really bad stuff. I remembered Carlos, how thin he was, and the dirt under his nails. I thought about Ledge and how nervous he seemed, with all those tics and twitches.

"Man," I said. "That's messed up."

"Yes, sir," said my brother. "But hey — Hey! Why are we talking about this negative stuff? I'm gonna tell Dad he's got a baller in the family!"

"Another one!" I said, because my brother was legit on the court.

He smacked me on the back. It wasn't a Yeti smack. It was an older brother smack. We both smiled.

"But let me tell him about the game first, okay?" I said.

"It's all you," said Junior.

"It's just that, I don't know, it's funny," I said. "It was like Dad knew I could do it before he even knew what *it* was."

"Yeah," he said. "He's funny that way."

After that, we walked along without saying much. That's easy to do when you'd spent years sharing a room with someone. You can just be in the same place with them, and be glad they're there, but not have to say anything.

And that made me think of my room. And that made me think of my history paper. So I was walking along, thinking about the paper and about the game, about the game and about the paper. All of a sudden, I knew the answer. I knew what Martin Luther King, Jr., meant to me.

"Hey, bro," I said. "I'll see you back there, all right?"

"Wait," he said. "Is Dad getting pizza? Ice cream? You know something?"

"Nah, nah," I said, laughing. "It's nothing like that. Just something I have to do."

I took off at a run.

• • •

"Hey, Dad!" I called as soon as I got through the front door. By the time he called "Hey, STAT!" back, I was already in my room. I flipped open my history notebook and began reading what I'd already written. And there it was, right in front of me.

Dr. King stood up for what he believed was right against tough odds, and I'd sort of done that, too. Of course, he was fighting for equal rights for all people, and I just thought it was wrong that some older kids were acting like jerks and kicking my friends and me off our home court. But, I mean, he was a reverend *and* had a PhD. I was eleven. You gotta start somewhere!

I started writing. I wrote about him organizing important marches and demonstrations and what that meant to me. This time I had an answer: One person could do a lot, but the more people you had behind you, the more you could accomplish. I thought about Mike and Deuce. How we'd worked together today to beat a bigger team. I thought about Junior helping out and all the kids who came to watch and how that helped us have a fair game.

127

"After a while, even bullies start behaving when they know people are watching," I wrote. "Dr. King knew it, and I can tell you for a fact that it's true."

I finished the last page in no time flat. Then I went out to talk to my dad. I thought that, all things considered, I might be able to talk him into getting some pizza tonight. Turns out, he wasn't too hard to convince!

Before I got to class the next day, I had double-checked the paper and was ready to go. Except for one spot where I'd sort of torn the page while erasing something, it looked really good. I'd put a lot of work into it, and I was looking forward to handing it in. I could already picture it coming back with a big "A" at the top. And when I pictured a little harder, I could even see a "+" on there. But I had one quick pit stop to make on the way to class.

CHAPTER 16

*A*fter school, I noticed my skateboard leaning against the wall in the corner of my room. With all the excitement on the b-ball court, I'd kind of been ignoring it. I took it out on the sidewalk, and before long I was skating to the little park. I spent a while over on the other side from the court doing the easy tricks I already knew. I worked my way up to the pop-shuvit and did my first really good one.

In the past, I probably would've stayed there until I really got the hang of it. Not today. I really was getting a little tall for this thing. And I realized something else, too: I missed my friends. And of course, I had a good idea where they were.

I got back on my board and headed for the court. Sure enough, they were there — and they weren't alone. Some of the kids who'd been there to cheer us on yesterday were out there in shorts and sneakers. People were passing a few old balls around and using both hoops, even the old bent one on the other side. As I was watching, Tavoris launched himself up and back in a crazy fadeaway jumper, just to try to get square with the bent-down rim.

With all the talking and joking around, I got closer than usual before anyone heard my skateboard. But Mike and Deuce recognized the sound as soon as they heard it.

"Hey, STAT," Mike called. "Get over here!"

I usually walked over from the sidewalk and left my board in the grass, but I tried something different this time. When I reached the little concrete walkway that led up to the court, I kick-turned my board and started rolling down the path. Now everyone could hear the wheels rumbling along underneath me. Even Marcus stopped talking long enough to turn and look.

Instead of getting off the board when I reached the court, I rolled right onto it. I clapped my hands once and held them up for Deuce. He smiled and fired a pass right to me. He even led me perfectly, as if he passed to guys on skateboards all the time. I grabbed the ball out of the air and kicked hard toward the good hoop. When I got there, I laid it up, underhand.

The ball bounced off the backboard and onto the rim. It rattled all the way around in one full circle. Finally, as I rolled past, the ball tipped and fell through the hoop.

"Traveling!" Deuce called.

Everyone laughed, especially me. He got me good on that one. I stashed the board over in the corner and then played some basketball. We just shot around at first.

"Brick!" I shouted as Deuce released an ugly-looking fadeaway.

"Clang!" shouted Mike as the ball hit the back rim and bounced straight up.

"Boo-ya!" called Deuce as the ball somehow came straight down and went through the hoop. "Just like I planned."

"Yeah, right!" Mike and I said at the same time.

After the battle we fought to get this court back, it felt good just to fool around and have some fun on it. I looked around and saw the whole court had been cleaned up. It probably didn't take long with so many kids to help out. And with no one fouling up the lawns anymore, my dad had come home early and in a good mood, too. Now that Carlos and his crew had been kicked off the court, they had no reason to come around here and mess the neighborhood up.

After that, Mike and I tried to dunk. Neither of us could quite get there yet, but I was getting close. I had one where I jammed the bottom of the ball against the rim — so close! I might have been getting a little tall for skating, but I was definitely getting to be the right size for hoops.

"Yo, guys!" someone called out.

It was Roger.

"Two-on-two?" he said.

"Sure," I said.

"Definitely," said Deuce.

"Just go easy on my back," said Mike.

"All right, old man," I said.

He didn't need to worry. It wasn't going to be that kind of game. We were just friends having fun. A few kids wanted to join in after a while, and we let them take our spots. Mike, Deuce, and I walked down to the sidewalk together. My board was under my arm, my friends were at my side, and my history paper was history.

Dad was right, I thought. *You can do it all.*

"Yo, space cadet," said Deuce, waving his hand in front of my face.

"Yeah?" I said, snapping back to the here and now.

"You think any more about that tournament?" he said.

"Oh, yeah," said Mike. "What about that? You sign up?"

"All the sign-up spots are gone," I said with a shrug.

"Are you sure?" said Deuce.

"Oh, yeah, I'm sure," I said. "I took the last one today."

We all started laughing.

"Awesome!" said Deuce. "You had us worried there for a second."

"Yeah, but I had to sign up," I said, looking at them both. "I have a great team."

AMAR'E WAS JUST GETTING WARMED UP.

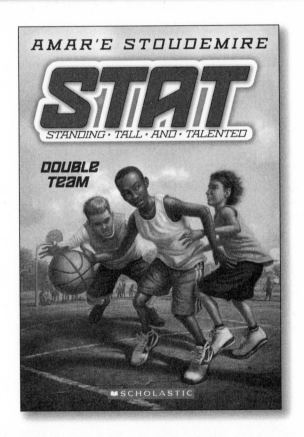

AMAR'E STOUDEMIRE

STAT
STANDING · TALL · AND · TALENTED

DOUBLE TEAM

SCHOLASTIC

NOW IT'S GAME TIME!

Here is an excerpt from the next book.

"Yeah, that was sweet," said Deuce. "But we need to keep working. These tourney teams can definitely play some D. And the one this weekend is the toughest yet."

"I'm on it," I said.

"Yeah, right," said Deuce, doing a quick, slick crossover dribble as he talked. "You barely even signed up for that first tournament."

"Yeah, and who was MVP of the last one?" I shot back.

I had him there. But Deuce was right, too. The teams we were playing now definitely knew their stuff. Whatever play we ran, they'd seen it before. And it sounded like the teams this weekend were going to be even better.

"All right, let's do this!" I said, clapping my hands twice.

"Hold up, hold up," Mike said.

I saw another kid edging onto the court. Deuce held the ball and we all turned toward this guy. He looked familiar. He was tall and thin and had a little forward lean to him, like a bendy straw. Then I remembered where I'd seen him. He was the new kid in our grade at school.

"Hey, Doug-AY!" called Mike.

Yeah, that was his name: Dougie. Deuce gave him a little wave, and he waved back. Then he headed over to where we were standing near the free throw line.

He had this complicated handshake that was like: fist bump, hook fingertips together, up tap, down tap, and another fist bump. I was surprised when Mike and Deuce both knew it. He turned to me last. His hand was out, ready for the fist bump, but I just nodded. I didn't catch all of the parts to their handshake and anyway that wasn't the kind of move I came here to work on.

Mike must've figured out what I was thinking because he said, "Dougie's been practicing with us while you were away. He's a good guy."

"Cool," I said. "I'm Amar'e."

"I know," he said. "I'm Dougie."

"I know," I said. We both smiled, but I still didn't shake his hand. I wasn't being mean: I still had no idea of the order!

Anyway, there were four of us now. I thought we should keep working on the pick-and-roll, with defenders on both players like in a real game. It got even more complicated with all that traffic coming together at one spot. But they all wanted to run two-on-two right away.

"Yeah, come on, STAT," said Deuce. "We worked on all that stuff the whole time you were gone."

That didn't help me much, I wanted to say, but I didn't mind playing two-on-two. I kind of wanted to see what Dougie could do other than bump fists. I'd get a close look, too, because he wound up being my teammate.

"He's a pretty good distributor," said Deuce, meaning he was a guard.

"All right," I said. "We get the ball first."

"Why do they call you STAT?" Dougie asked as we waited for Mike and Deuce to line up and check the ball back to us.

"It's kind of a nickname," I said. "My dad gave it to me. It means Standing Tall and Talented. It's like, part nickname and part reminder."

"Cool," he said.

Dougie played with the same forward lean he had when he walked. His head was always a little in front of his body. It made him look kind of like he was trying to read an eye chart, but it gave him a wicked head fake. Deuce bit on one right off the bat, and Dougie snuck by him and laid it in to give us an early lead.

We were playing make it, take it, because the trash talk was better that way, and I scored the next bucket. I got decent position down low. Then Dougie bounced the ball to me and I worked Mike over with a quick up-and-under move. It was harder than usual because of Mike's new size. He'd grown a lot in the last few months, though most of it was sideways. Just like that, we were up 2–0.

It was a pretty good game after that.